D1504883

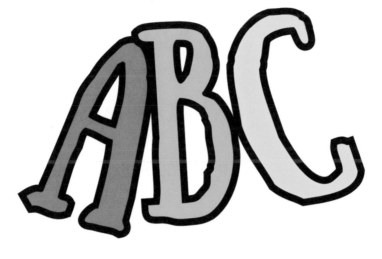

Book of Silly Food

By K Emory Taylor

Copyright © 2024 by Katherine A. Taylor

All rights reserved. No part of this book may be used or reproduced in any manner whatsoever without written permission. For more information go to poetryfrogillustrations@gmail.com

To all the kids who read this book, and to the parents who buy this book.
I hope this book makes you hungry and inspires you to
eat more fruit and veggies!

A Asparagus

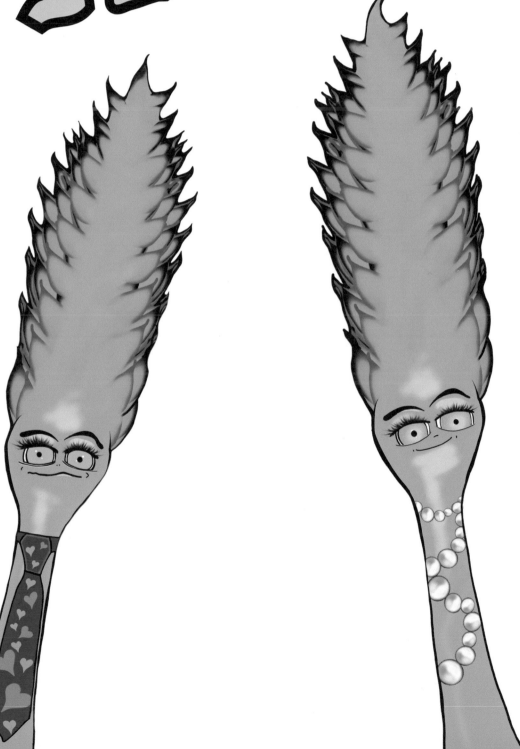

B Blueberry

Broccoli

C Carrot

E Eggplant

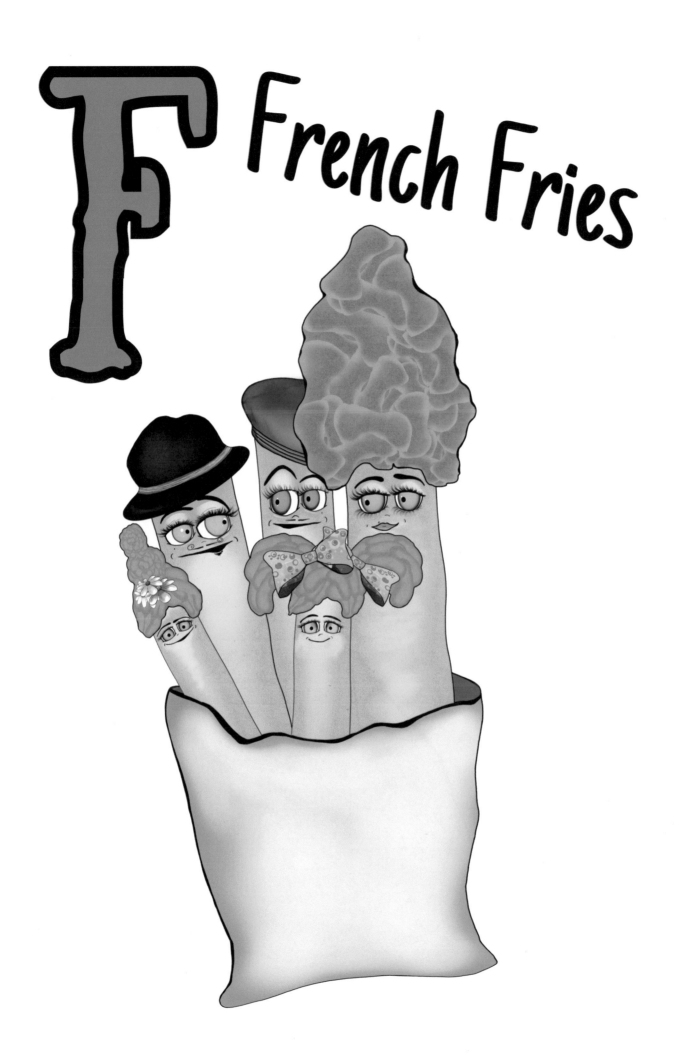

F French Fries

G Garlic

Grapefruit

H Habaneros

I Iceberg Lettuce

Ice Cream

J

Jack Fruit

K Kobocha Squash

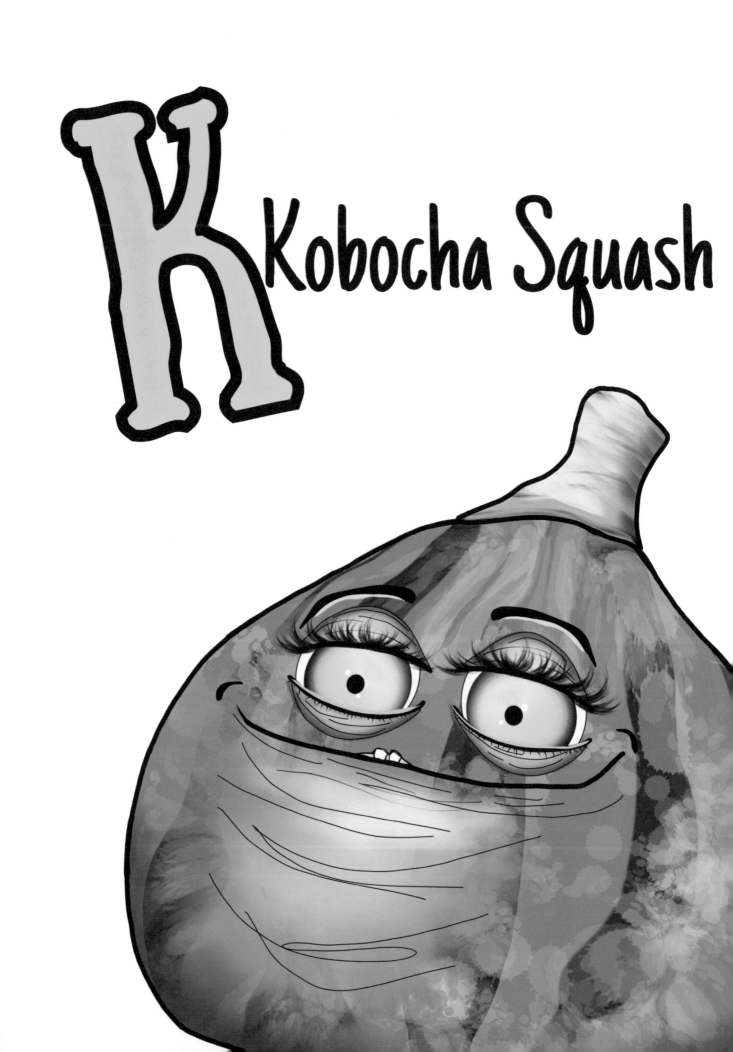

L Lemon

Mango

Macaroni & Cheese

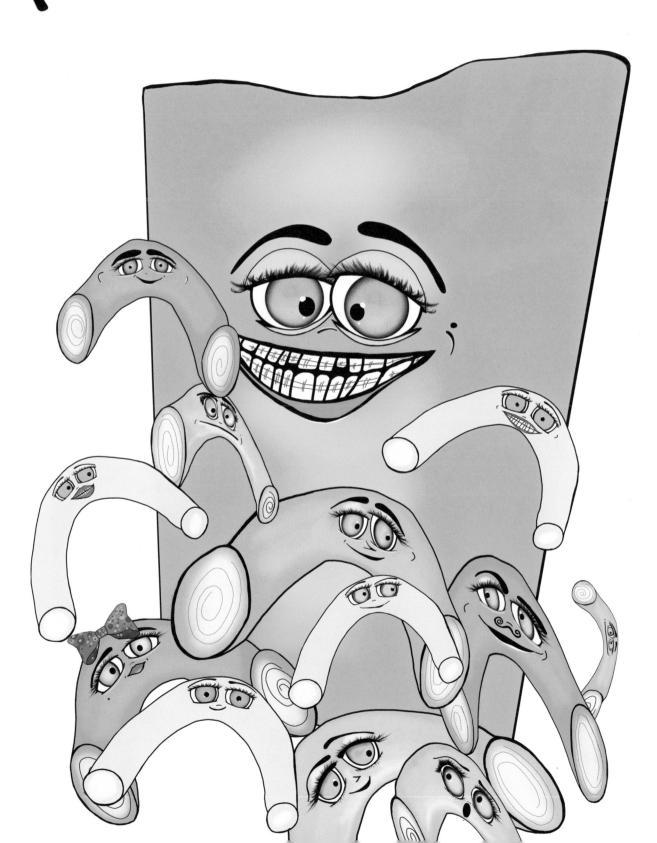

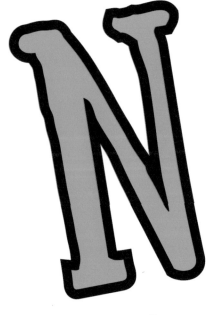

Nachos

Nectarine

O Olive

P Potato

Peas

Pretzel Pizza

Peanut Butter
and Jelly

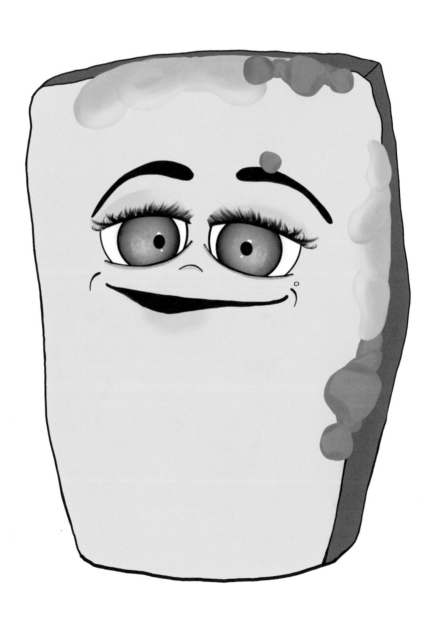

Q Quince

R

Radish

S Sweet Potatoes

T Tangerine

Taco

U Uglie Fruit

W

Watermelon

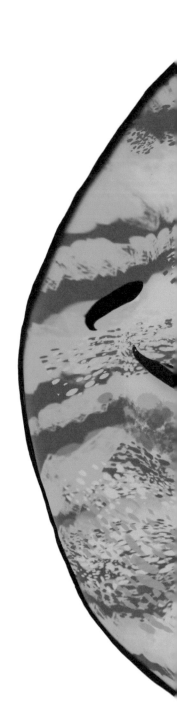

X

Ximenia

Y

Yumberry

Z

Zebra Melon

Zucchini

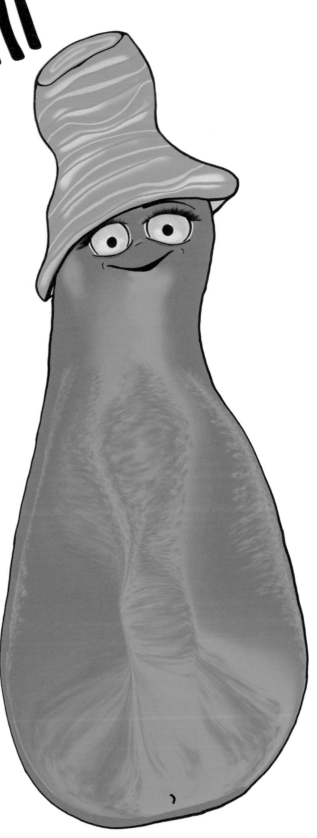

Zeppole

ABCDEFG
HIJKLMNO
PQRSTUV
WXYZzzzzz

Let's Sing the Alphabet –

Asparagus, Blueberry, Broccoli, Carrot, Donut,

STOP Dragon my Fruit

Egggplant, French Fries, Grapefruit, Habaneros,

Iceberg Lettuce, Ice Cream, Jack Fruit,

Kabocha Squash, Lemmmmon,

Macaroni & Cheese

Mango, Nachos, Olive, Potato, Peas, Pizza, Pretzel

Peanut Butter & Jelllllly

Radish, Sweet Potatoes, Tangerine,

Taco, Uglie Fruit, Victoria Plum,

Watermelon

Ximenia, Yumberry, Zebra Melon,

Zeppole!

The End - I am hungry, let's eat!!

Made in United States
Troutdale, OR
05/21/2024

20047116R00031